I0815349

SPACE OBJECTS

THE SUN

by Elizabeth Andrews

Cody Koala
An Imprint of Pop!
popbooksonline.com

Hello! My name is Cody Koala

This book is filled with videos, puzzles, games, and more! Scan the QR codes* while you read, or visit the website below to make this book pop.

popbooksonline.com/sun

*Scanning QR codes requires a web-enabled smart device with a QR code reader app and a camera.

abdobooks.com

Published by Pop!, a division of ABDO, PO Box 398166, Minneapolis, Minnesota 55439.

Printed in the United States of America, North Mankato, Minnesota.

102024
012025

Cover Photo: Shutterstock Images
Interior Photos: Getty Images, NASA, Shutterstock Images
Editor: Grace Hansen
Series Designer: Victoria Bates

Library of Congress Control Number: 2024938604

Publisher's Cataloging-in-Publication Data

Names: Andrews, Elizabeth, author.
Title: The sun / by Elizabeth Andrews
Description: Minneapolis, Minnesota : Pop!, 2025 | Series: Space objects | Includes online resources and index
Identifiers: ISBN 9781098247003 (lib. bdg.) | ISBN 9781098247560 (ebook)
Subjects: LCSH: Outer space--Exploration--Juvenile literature. | Sun--Juvenile literature. | Stars--Juvenile literature. | Solar system--Juvenile literature. | Astronomy--Juvenile literature. | Universe--Juvenile literature.
Classification: DDC 523.7--dc23

Table of Contents

Chapter 1
The Sun's Beginning 4

Chapter 2
Main Sequence Star 8

Chapter 3
Orbiting Bodies 12

Chapter 4
The Sun and Earth 16

Making Connections 22
Glossary 23
Index 24
Online Resources 24

Chapter 1

The Sun's Beginning

The Sun is a star. It is the closest star to Earth. The Sun began forming 4.6 billion years ago. Its life started in a giant spinning cloud of gas and dust called a nebula.

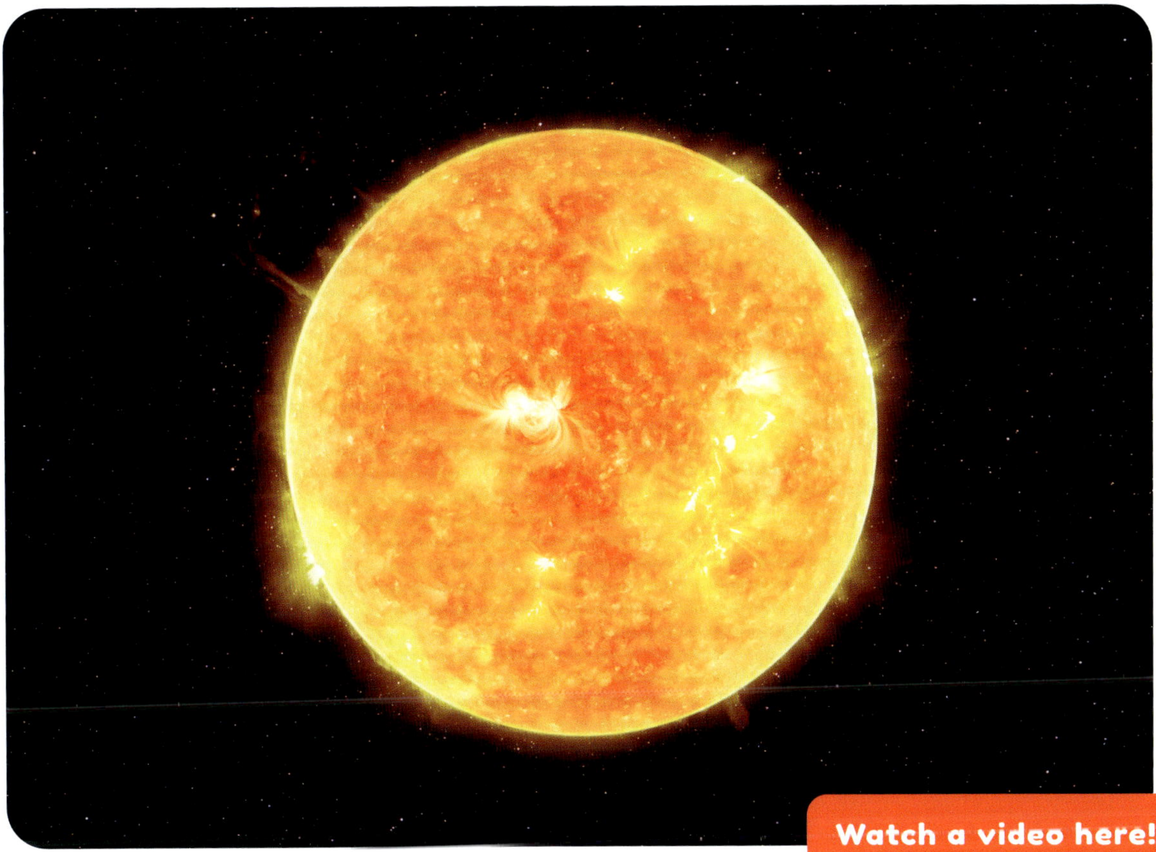

nebula

Watch a video here!

Over millions of years, gas and dust clumped together inside the nebula. A **dense core** formed from the collected materials. The clump became a protostar. The Sun was born!

Chapter 2

Main Sequence Star

As a protostar, the Sun continued to spin, pull in more materials, and get hotter. Its **core** got so hot, **nuclear fusion** began. Hydrogen gas turned into helium gas.

Learn more here!

Nuclear fusion gives the Sun energy. Today, the Sun is a main sequence star. It uses energy from its core to shine.

The Sun, like all stars, will spend 90% of its life as a main sequence star.

Scientists believe the Sun will be a main sequence star for another 5.5 billion years.

Chapter 3

Orbiting Bodies

The Sun is not solid. It is a large spinning ball of gas and dust. The Sun sits at the center of our **solar system**. Eight planets and other space objects **orbit** the Sun.

asteroid

Neptune

constellation

Uranus

Jupiter

Mars

Saturn

Venus

Mercury

Earth

Sun

Explore links here!

Our solar system is in the Milky Way galaxy. A galaxy is a collection of billions of stars and other matter held

together by **gravity**. The Sun orbits the center of the Milky Way galaxy.

Chapter 4

The Sun and Earth

The Sun is 864,000 miles (1.4 million km) wide and is made up of layers. The Sun's **temperature** varies. Its hottest point is in its **core**, which is 27 million °F (15 million °C)!

According to scientists, 1.3 million Earths could fit inside the Sun.
Complete an activity here!
Earth to scale

THE STRUCTURE OF THE SUN

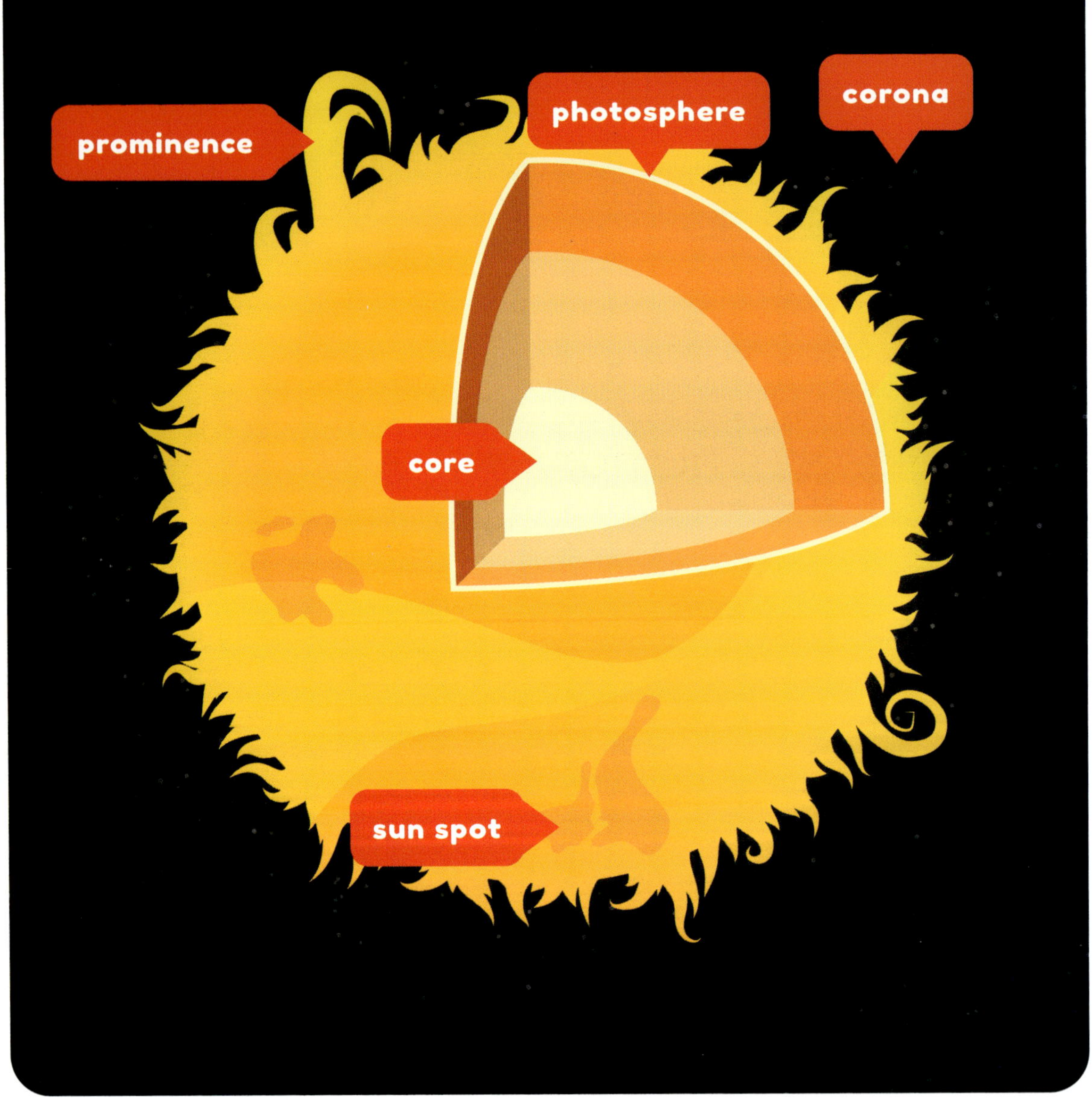

The Sun has different layers. The photosphere is the Sun's surface. This is what humans see. The photosphere is 10,000°F (5,500°C). The corona can be more than 3 million °F (2 million °C).

The Earth depends on the Sun to support life. The Sun's light and heat gives the Earth energy.

This energy helps plants grow and water remain liquid. Air heated by the Sun makes wind.

Making Connections

Text-to-Self

What is your favorite and least favorite thing about the Sun? Explain your answers.

Text-to-Text

Have you read any books about other space objects? If so, how were those objects similar to or different from the Sun?

Text-to-World

How would life be different if the Sun was hotter or colder?

Glossary

core – the center of an object.

dense – having parts very close together with little space between.

gravity – a force that pulls objects toward each other.

nuclear fusion – a process that happens when two nuclei join to form a single nucleus.

orbit – the path of a space object as it moves around another space object. To orbit is to follow this path.

solar system – the group of planets and other space objects that revolve around the Sun and are held together by the Sun's gravity.

temperature – how much heat is in something.

Index

core, 7–8, 10, 16

corona, 19

Earth, 4, 20

gas, 4, 7–8, 12

main sequence star, 10–11

Milky Way, 14–15

nebula, 4, 7

photosphere, 19

protostar, 7–8

solar system, 12, 14

temperature, 16, 19

wind, 21

Online Resources

popbooksonline.com

Thanks for reading this Cody Koala book!

This book is filled with videos, puzzles, games, and more! Scan the QR codes* while you read, or visit the website below to make this book pop.

popbooksonline.com/sun

*Scanning QR codes requires a web-enabled smart device with a QR code reader app and a camera.